I0118783

National Steeplechase Association

Members, Certificate of Incorporation, By-Laws, Rules of Racing

National Steeplechase Association

Members, Certificate of Incorporation, By-Laws, Rules of Racing

ISBN/EAN: 9783337419967

Printed in Europe, USA, Canada, Australia, Japan

Cover: Foto ©Suzi / pixelio.de

More available books at **www.hansebooks.com**

NATIONAL
STEEPLECHASE ASSOCIATION.

ORGANIZED, JANUARY 4th, 1895.

INCORPORATED, FEBRUARY 18th, 1895.

MEMBERS,
CERTIFICATE OF INCORPORATION,
BY-LAWS,
RULES OF RACING.

OFFICERS.

President, AUGUST BELMONT,

Vice-President, H. DECOURCY FORBES.

Treasurer and Honorary Secretary, S. S. HOWLAND,

Secretary, H. G. CRICKMORE.

STEWARDS.

To serve one year :	*To serve two years :*	*To serve three years :*
AUGUST BELMONT,	A. J. CASSATT,	H. DECOURCY FORBES,
F. H. PRINCE,	FOXHALL KEENE,	J. O. GREEN,
J. G. FOLLANSBEE.	S. S. HOWLAND.	F. GEBHARD.

NEW YORK :

J. J. O'BRIEN & SON, PRINTERS AND STATIONERS, 122 EAST 23D STREET.

1895.

MEMBERS.

A

ALEXANDRE, JOHN E........................N. Y.
ALEXANDRE, J. H..........................N. Y.
ALLEN, PHILIP.............................N. Y.
ALTEMUS, L. C............................Penn.
ASTOR, J. J...............................N. Y.

B

BARNES, JOHN S...........................N. Y.
BARTLETT, Hon. FRANKLIN..................N. Y.
BEARD, FRANCIS D.........................N. Y.
BEARD, J ROBINSON........................N. Y.
BELMONT, AUGUST..........................N. Y.
BELMONT, O. H. P.........................R I.
BELMONT, PERRY...........................N. Y.
BERESFORD, JOHN G........................N. Y.
BIRD, O. W...............................N. Y.
BOWERS, JOHN M...........................N. Y.
BRADFORD, J. H..........................Mass.
BROWN, ALEX...............................Md.
BROWN, JESSE.............................D. C.
BROWN, NEILSON..........................Penn.
BUCK, H. A...............................N. Y.
BUCKLEY, JULIAN G........................N. Y.

C

CAMERON, BENNEHAN........................N. C.
CANER, HARRISON K.......................Penn.
CARMAN, RICHARD..........................N. Y.
CARROLL, ROYAL PHELPS....................N. Y.
CASE, H. P...............................N. Y.
CASSATT, A. J...........................Penn.
CLARKE, JOSEPH............................Cal.
CLASON, AUGUSTUS.........................N. Y.
CLYDE, B. F.............................Penn.
CLYDE, THOMAS............................N. Y.
COLLIER, P. F............................N. Y.
COSTER, CHARLES..........................N. Y.
CURTIS, DR. HOLBROOK.....................N. Y.

D

Davis, E. W.................................R. I.
Donner, J. O.............................N. Y.
Dulany, H. Rozier..........................D. C.

E

Elliott, Duncan...........................N. Y.
Ellis, R. N...............................N. Y.
Ellis, W. S...............................Penn.
Eustis, George............................D. C.
Eustis, W. C..............................D. C.

F

Fairfax, Henry............................Va.
Follansbee, John G........................Cal.
Forbes, H. DeCourcy.......................N. Y.

G

Galway, James.............................N. Y.
Gebhard, F................................N. J.
Gould, George J...........................N. J.
Green, Dr. J. O...........................Ky.
Griscom, Clement A........................Penn.
Griswold, F. Gray.........................N. Y.
Guliver, W. C.............................N. Y.

H

Haggin, J. B..............................Cal.
Harrison, Mitchell........................Penn.
Havemeyer, C. F...........................N. Y.
Hearst, W. R..............................Cal.
Heckscher, J. G...........................N. Y.
Herbert, H. L.............................N. Y.
Hill, Dr. Richard S.......................Md.
Hitch, F. D...............................N. Y.
Hitchcock, Center.........................N. Y.
Howland, S. S.............................N. Y.
Hunter, John..............................N. Y.

I

Iselin, C. Oliver.........................N. Y.

J

JOHNSON, Capt. F. G......................Canada.
JONES, FRANK W...........................Mass.

K

KANE, DELANCEY.......................... ....N. Y.
KEENE, FOXHALL P..........................N. Y.
KEENE, JAMES R............................N. Y.
KENNEDY, H. VAN RENSSELAER.................N. Y.
KELLY, EDWARD ....N. Y.
KIP, LAWRENCE.............................N. Y.
KIRKMAN, V. L.............................Tenn.
KNAPP, Dr. G. LEE..........................N. Y.

L

LA MONTAGNE, E. C...................... ...N. Y.
LAWRENCE, J. G. K..........................N. Y.
LAWRENCE, PRESCOTT.........................N. Y.
LENT. EUGENE.............................. ....Cal.
LOGAN, JOHN A............ ....D. C.
LORILLARD, PIERRE, JR.......................N. Y.

Mc

McCULLOUGH, E. H..........................Penn.
McDONALD, CHARLES B.........................Ill.
MACDONOUGH, W. O'B..... ....Cal.
McKAY, TWOMBLY HAMILTON ....N. J.
McLEAN, JOHN R............. ....D. C.

M

MACKEY, F. J...............................Ill.
MADDOX, JAMES K...........................Va.
MAITLAND, THOMAS A........................N. Y.
MATTHER, C. E.............................Penn.
MILLS, OGDEN..............................N. Y.
MOORE, CLARANCE...........................D. C.
MORGAN, J. PIERPONT.......................N. Y.
MORRELL, EDWARD DE V.....................Penn.
MORRIS, A. NEWBOLD ....N. Y.
MORRIS, HENRY J...........................Penn.
MORTIMER, RICHARD.........................N. Y.
MUNN, H. N...............................N. Y.
MURPHY, DANIEL..... ....Cal.
MURPHY, DANIEL...........................N. Y.

O

OELRICHS, HERMANN........................N. Y.
O'RIELLY, F. C............................N. J.

P

PALMER, RICHARD S.........................N. Y.
PERRIN, CLIFFORD..........................Ohio
PETERS, RICHARD...........................N. Y.
PFIZER, CHARLES, JR.......................N. Y.
POLLOCK, GEORGE...........................N. Y.
POTTER, E. C..............................N. Y.
PRINCE, F. H..............................Mass.

R

RANDOLPH, EDMUND..........................N. Y.
RANDOLPH, P. S. P.........................Penn.
RATHBONE, J. L............................Cal.
RIDDLE, S. D..............................Penn.
RIDDLE, L. W..............................Penn.
ROBBINS, S. HOWLAND.......................N. Y.
ROBY, E. WILLARD..........................N. Y.
RUPPERT, J., JR...........................N. Y.

S

SANFORD, JOHN.............................N. Y.
SCHERMERHORN, AUG.........................N. Y.
SMITH, SIDNEY J...........................N. Y.
STEWARD, JOHN A. JR.......................N. Y.
STRATHY, Col. J. A. L.....................Canada.

T

TAILER, W. H..............................N. Y.
THAYER, BAYARD............................Mass.
THOMPSON, L. S............................N. J.
THOMPSON, W. P............................N. J.
THOMPSON, W. P., JR.......................N. J.
TOWNSEND, ISAAC...........................N. Y.
TOWNSEND, J. R............................N. Y.

V

VAN BRUNT, R............................Cal.
VANDERBILT, CORNELIUS.....................N. Y.
VINGUT, H. K.............................N. J.

W

WADSWORTH, CRAIG W......................N. Y.
WADSWORTH, JAMES S......................N. Y.
WALCOTT, A. F...........................N. Y.
WARBURTON, BARCLAY H....................Penn.
WEBB, CREIGHTON.........................N. Y.
WEBB, SEWARD............................Vt.
WETMORE, Hon. G. PEABODY................R. I.
WHITE, STANFORD.........................N. Y.
WIDENER, JOSEPH E.......................Penn.
WILLIAMS, THOS. H., JR..................Cal.
WINTHROP, R. D..........................N. Y.
WORK, GEORGE............................N. Y.

CERTIFICATE OF INCORPORATION

— OF —

NATIONAL STEEPLECHASE ASSOCIATION.

We, AUGUST BELMONT, of Hempstead, Queens County, New York, H. DeCOURCY FORBES, of New York City, New York, SAMUEL S. HOWLAND, of Groveland, Livingston County, New York, JAMES O. GREEN, of Louisville, Kentucky, and FREDERICK GEBHARD, of Eatontown, Monmouth County, New Jersey, all being of full age and citizens of the United States of America and a majority being residents of the State of New York, desiring to form a corporation pursuant to the provisions of Chapter 213 of the Laws of 1891, the same being an Act of the Legislature of the State of New York, passed April 20, 1891. entitled "An Act to provide for the formation of Corporations for Improving the Breeds of Domestic Animals," *Do Hereby Certify.*

FIRST: The name by which the corporation shall be known is "National Steeplechase Association."

SECOND: The particular objects and purposes of said corporation are as follows: The investigating, ascertaining and keeping of a record of the pedigrees of horses; the instituting, maintaining, controlling and publishing of a stud book or book of registry of horses in the United States of America and Canada; the promoting and holding of exhibitions of such horses; and generally for the purposes of improving the breed thereof, by encouraging and advancing steeplechasing and hurdle racing throughout the

United States, by supervising such races, by compiling, publishing and enforcing of proper rules to govern such racing, by licensing of meetings, of trainers and of jockeys, and by such other means as may be proper.

THIRD: The number of Directors who shall manage the affairs of said corporation shall be nine.

FOURTH: The first Annual Meeting of the members of the corporation shall be held on the 9th day of January, 1896.

FIFTH: The names and places of residence of the Directors who shall manage the affairs of the corporation until such first Annual Meeting, are as follows:

Names:	Places of Residence:
AUGUST BELMONT, . .	Hempstead, Queens County, New York.
H. DeCOURCY FORBES,	New York City, New York.
SAMUEL S. HOWLAND, .	Groveland, Livingston County, New York.
JAMES O. GREEN, . .	Louisville, Kentucky.
FREDERICK GEBHARD, .	Eatontown, New Jersey.
A. J. CASSATT, . . .	Haverford, Pennsylvania.
FOXHALL P. KEENE, .	Bayside, New York.
JOHN G. FOLLANSBEE, .	San Francisco, California.
FREDERICK H. PRINCE,	Boston, Massachusetts.

SIXTH: The principal office of said corporation is to be located in the City and County of New York.

IN WITNESS WHEREOF, we have made, signed, acknowledged and filed this Certificate.

Dated, New York, February 15th, 1895.

> AUGUST BELMONT,
> H. DeC. FORBES,
> S. S. HOWLAND,
> J. O. GREEN,
> F. GEBHARD.

STATE OF NEW YORK,   } ss.

CITY AND COUNTY OF NEW YORK. }

On this 16th day of February, 1895, before me personally appeared August Belmont, to me personally known and known to me to be one of the individuals described in and who made and signed the foregoing Certificate, and he duly acknowledged to me that he had made, signed and executed the same for the purposes therein set forth.

EDWARD CORNELL.

[SEAL]   *Notary Public,*

Orange County.

Certificate filed in New York County.

STATE OF NEW YORK,   } ss.

CITY AND COUNTY OF NEW YORK. }

On this 15th day of February, 1895, before me personally appeared H. DeCourcy Forbes, Samuel S. Howland, James O. Green and Frederick Gebhard, to me personally known and known to me to be four of the individuals described in and who made and signed the foregoing Certificate, and they severally duly acknowledged to me that they had made, signed and executed the same for the purposes therein set forth.

EDWARD L. PURDY,

[SI AL.]   *Notary Public,* (148),

N. Y. Co.

STATE OF NEW YORK,   } ss.

OFFICE OF THE SECRETARY OF STATE. }

I have compared the preceding with the original Certificate of Incorporation of National Steeplechase Association filed and recorded in this office on the

18th day of February, 1895, and do hereby certify the same to be a correct transcript therefrom and of the whole of said original.

WITNESS my hand and the seal of office of the Secretary of State, at the city of Albany, this 18th day of February, one thousand eight hundred and ninety-five.

JNO. PALMER,

[SEAL.]   *Secretary of State.*

STATE OF NEW YORK,   }
                                      } *ss.*
CITY AND COUNTY OF NEW YORK.   }

I, HENRY D. PURROY, Clerk of the said City and County, and Clerk of the Supreme Court of said State for said County, *Do Certify*, that I have compared the preceding with the original Certificate of Incorporation of National Steeplechase Association on file in my office, and that the same is a correct transcript therefrom, and of the whole of such original.

Endorsed, Filed and Recorded February 19th, 1895, 9 H. 57 M.

IN WITNESS WHEREOF, I have hereunto subscribed my name and affixed my official seal, this 19th day of February, 1895.

HENRY D. PURROY,

[SEAL.]   *Clerk.*

[ENDORSED]

Certificate of Incorporation of National Steeplechase Association.

STATE OF NEW YORK,   }
                                    }
OFFICE OF SECRETARY OF STATE.   }

Filed and Recorded February 18th, 1895.

ANDREW DAVIDSON,
Deputy Secretary of State.

BY·LAWS

OF

NATIONAL STEEPLECHASE ASSOCIATION.

Reported to the Stewards by the Committee, H. De Courcy Forbes and Dr. J. O. Green, and adopted March 4, 1895.

BOARD OF STEWARDS.

1.—The Directors of the Corporation shall also be the Stewards of the Association, and whenever the word Steward is used in these By-Laws it shall be taken and held to include the term Director. Of the nine Stewards named as Directors in the Certificate of Incorporation, three shall serve for one year, three for two years and three for three years, their names to be determined by lot. The first year shall be taken and held to terminate on the 9th day of January, 1896.

2.—Vacancies in the Board of Stewards occurring during the year shall be filled for the unexpired term by a majority vote of the remaining members of the Board at any regular meeting of the Board, or at any special meeting called for the purpose of filling such vacancies.

3.—The Board of Stewards shall meet on the first Thursday of every month, and whenever called together by the Secretary, at the request of the President, or in his absence, the Vice-President, or of any two of the Stewards. Five members of the Board shall constitute a quorum for the transaction of business.

4.—The Board of Stewards shall annually elect from among its own members, a President, Vice-President and Treasurer. It shall also annually elect from among its own members, or from among the other members of the Association, a Secretary and such other officers, officials and committees as it may deem necessary.

5. (I.)—The Board of Stewards shall have full and complete control of all the affairs of the Association; it shall make, publish and enforce rules for racing, the conduct of meetings, the licensing of trainers, jockeys and gentlemen riders, etc.; it shall fix and may alter the amounts of initiation fees and dues to be paid by the members; it shall appoint and remove Deputy Stewards, officers and officials, and generally conduct the affairs of the Association.

5. (II)—As incidental to and part of the powers above mentioned, the Board of Stewards shall have power to recognize any Association which shall adopt rules conforming to those of this Association for the management and control of races to be held by Hunt Clubs, Country Clubs or approved members of the same, with the sanction of the Governors of their respective Clubs.

6. (I.)—The Board of Stewards may appoint from its own members an Executive Committee to consist of five members, and such Committee may exercise, in the intervals between meetings of the Board of Stewards, all of the powers of such Board.

(II.)—Three members of the Executive Commmittee shall constitute a quorum for the transaction of business at any meeting of the Committee. The Executive Committee shall keep minutes of all of its action and proceedings, and such action and proceedings shall be, from time to time, reported to the Board of Stewards at the meetings of such Board, and the minutes of the Executive Committee shall be read at such meetings of the Board.

7.—The funds of the Association shall be devoted solely to the purposes for which the Association was incorporated, and no part thereof shall at any time be divided among its members, and in case of the dissolution of the Association shall be devoted to such uses for the purposes of improving the breed of horses as the Stewards shall determine.

MEETINGS OF THE ASSOCIATION.

8. (I.)—The Annual Meeting of the Association shall be held on the first Thursday after the first Monday in January in each year, at such time and place as the Board of Stewards may select.

(II)—In case a quorum cannot be obtained at any Annual Meeting, such meeting may be adjourned for a period not exceeding one month. If at any Annual Meeting or at an adjournment thereof no Stewards be elected to fill the places of those whose terms of office shall have expired, the latter shall continue to hold office and discharge the duties thereof until the election of their successors.

(III.)—It shall be the duty of the Secretary of the Association to mail to each member thereof, at least fourteen days prior to the date of the meeting, a notice of said meeting and the place and hour at which it will be held.

9.—The Secretary shall keep a book with the post-office addresses of members of the Association, and members must see that the addresses therein entered are their correct ones.

10.—At each annual meeting of the members of the Association three Stewards shall be elected by a majority vote of the members present in person or by proxy, to hold office for three years, and to fill the places of those whose term of office shall have expired.

11.—A quorum at an annual meeting shall consist of not less than one-fifth in number of the members of the Association, present in person, or represented by proxy, and in no case shall consist of less than nine members of the Association, present in person or represented by proxy.

SPECIAL MEETINGS.

12.—A Special Meeting of the Association may be called at any time by the Stewards, and shall be called by the President on the written application of one-third of the members of the Association.

13. (I.)—All notices of special meetings shall contain the subjects to be considered thereat, and none other shall be acted upon.

(II.)—All notices for special meetings shall be sent out by the Secretary, in the same manner as the notices of the annual meeting.

14.—A quorum at a special meeting of the Association shall be governed by the conditions of By-Law No. 11.

ELECTION OF MEMBERS.

15.—The members of the Association shall be the original incorporators, together with the Directors named in the

Certificate of Incorporation and such other persons as may from time to time, be duly elected to membership and qualify as such pursuant to the provisions of the By-Laws.

16. (I.)—All applications for membership must be proposed and seconded in writing by members of the Association.

(II.) The name of the applicant together with the names of his proposer and seconder, must be posted in the Secretary's office for at least ten days before it can be acted upon by the Stewards of the Association.

(III.) All members must be elected by a unanimous vote of the Board of Stewards. The name of a person whose application for membership has been rejected, cannot again be presented within twelve months.

(IV.) The initiation fees and dues of all members elected must be paid within fifteen days of the date of their election, or said election may be cancelled by the Board of Stewards.

17.—All subscriptions and dues shall be payable in advance on the 15th day of January in each year. The annual dues shall be $25. All members elected after the 1st day of May, 1895, shall be required to pay an initiation fee of $50.

18. Any member of the Association failing to pay his yearly dues or subscription by the first day of Apıil following, shall cease to be a member.

EXPULSION OF MEMBERS.

19. (I.)—In case the conduct of any member of the Association shall, in the opinion of the Board of Stewards, or of any twenty members of the Association (who shall certify the same to the Board of Stewards in writing), be considered

injurious to the Association, the Board of Stewards shall be especially summoned to consider the case, and should they find the charge proven, they may call upon the member to resign, or dismiss or expel him.

(II.) Such decision of the Board of Stewards shall be without appeal.

AMENDMENTS.

20. These By-Laws, with the exception of By-Law 7, may be amended at any meeting of the Board of Stewards by a majority vote. provided that ten days notice of the proposed amendment shall have been given to each member of the Board, or at any annual or special meeting of the Association, by a majority vote of the members of the Association ; provided, however, that, in such case, a written notice of such proposed amendment be mailed to each member of the Association, at least two weeks prior to the holding of the meeting at which it is to be considered, and that a copy thereof be posted on the bulletin board of the Association in the office of the Secretary, for the same period. But By-Law 7 shall not be amended, except by a unanimous vote of all the members of the Board of Stewards, or by unanimous vote of all the members of the Association, present in person, or represented by proxy, at any annual or special meeting of the Association, due notice having been given as above provided, that such a proposed amendment would be presented at such meeting.

Rules of Racing.

These rules apply to all meetings held under the
sanction of the NATIONAL STEEPLECHASE ASSOCIATION
and to all races run at such meetings.

PART I.

INTERPRETATION OF WORDS AND PHRASES.

1.   (I.) In the New England States and the States of *Recognized*
New York, New Jersey, Pennsylvania, Delaware, *Meetings.*
Maryland, Virginia and the District of Columbia,
a recognized meeting is a meeting held under the
sanction of the National Steeplechase Association,
the Jockey Club or the National Hunt Association.

(II.) A recognized meeting held in any part of the
United States, excepting the States named above
and the District of Columbia, is a meeting held
under the sanction of the American Turf Congress,
or a Turf Authority having a reciprocal agreement
with the National Steeplechase Association for
the mutual enforcement of sentences passed upon
persons guilty of fraudulent practices on the turf.

(III.) A recognized meeting held in any foreign
country is a meeting held under a Turf Authority of
the country in which it is held having a reciprocal
agreement with the American Steeplechase Association for the mutual enforcement of sentences
passed upon persons guilty of fraudulent practices
on the turf.

Wherever the word "Steward" or "Stewards" *Stewards.*
only is used, it means Steward or Stewards of the
meeting, or their duly appointed deputy or
deputies.

The "Registry Office" is the office for the time *Registry Office.*
being appointed as the Registry Office by the
Stewards of the National Steeplechase Association.
"Registered" and "Registration" mean *Registered and*
"registered," and "Registration" at such office. *Registration.*
(N. B.) The present Registry Office is the
Office of the Secretary of the National Steeplechase
Association.

Is such publication as the Stewards of the Na- *Racing*
tional Steeplechase Association shall designate. *Calendar.*

(N B The *spirit of the Times* is so designated.)

The "Forfeit List" is a record of arrears which *Forfeit List*
have been notified by the Clerk of the Course of
any meeting held under these rules, or by the
Registry Office of the Jockey Club or the National
Hunt Association, and by any Turf Authority
having a reciprocal agreement with the National
Steeplechase Association for the mutual enforcement of forfeits.

A "Horse" includes mare, gelding, colt and *Horse.*
filly.

A maiden is a horse which has never won a race *Maiden.*
(other than a match or private sweepstakes) in any
country. A Maiden means a maiden at the time
of the start.

A "Race" means purse, sweepstakes, private *Race.*
sweepstakes, cup or match.

A "Purse" is a race to be run for money or *Purse.*
other prize, without any stake being made by the
owners of the horses engaged and which is void if
two horses in entirely different interests are not
entered for it.

A "sweepstakes" is a race in which stakes are to *Sweepstakes.*
be made by the owners of the horses engaged, and
any such race is still a sweepstakes when money or
other prize is added.

A public sweepstakes is void if three subscribers do not engage horses in it.

A private sweepstakes is one to which no money
is added and which has not been advertised previous to closing.

A "cup" is any prize not given in money. *Cup.*

A "handicap" is a race in which the weights to *Handicap.*
be carried by the horses are adjusted by the handicapper for the purpose of equalizing their chances
of winning.

A "free handicap" is one in which no liability *Free Handicap.*
is incurred for entrance money, stake or forfeit,
until acceptance of the weight, either directly or
through omission to declare out.

A "private handicap" is one in which the *Private Handicap.*
weights are agreed upon among the parties to it,
and which has not been publicly advertised previous to the engagement being made.

A "post race" is one in which the subscribers *Post Race.*
declare at the usual time before a race for declar-
ing to start, the horse or horses they are to run,
without other limitation of choice than the rules of
racing and the conditions of the race prescribe.

A "produce race" is one to be run by the pro- *Produce Race.*
duce of horses named or described at the time of
entry.

A "selling race" is one, the conditions of which *Selling Race.*
require that every horse running, if a loser, may
be claimed, and if the winner must be offered for
sale by auction.

Weight for age means standard weight according *Weight for Age.*
to the rules of the course where the race is run or
its conditions, and remains a weight for age race
even though there be penalties and allowances.

A race at "catch weights" means one for which *Catch Weights.*
the riders need not weigh before or after the race.

The "nominator" is the person in whose name *Nominator.*
a horse is entered for a race.

"Owner" includes part owner or lessee. *Owner.*

"Authorized Agent" means an agent ap- *Authorized Agent.*
pointed by a document signed by the owner, and
lodged at the Registry Office, or, if for a single
meeting only, with the Clerk of the Course for
transmission to the Registry Office. Authorized
agent includes sub-agent, if authority to appoint a
sub-agent is provided for by the document.

"Arrears" are any sums unpaid in respect of *Arrears.*
fines, fees, entrance money, stakes, subscriptions,

forfeits and purchase money in races with selling allowances.

It is a "walk-over" when only one horse or *Walk-over.* horses belonging to a single interest are at the post ready to start for a race at the appointed time.

PART II.

CALCULATION OF TIME.

2.   (I.) When the last day for doing anything under *Dates falling on* these rules falls on Sunday, it may be done on the *Sunday.* following Monday, unless a race to which such act relates is appointed for that day, in which case it must be done on the previous Saturday.

    (II.) A "month" means a calendar month; a *Month and Day.* "day" means twenty-four hours.

PART III.

REGULATIONS FOR RACE MEETINGS.

3.   (I) All meetings held under these rules in the *Meetings must be* New England States and in the States of New York, *Sanctioned.* New Jersey, Pennsylvania, Delaware, Maryland and Virginia, and the District of Columbia, must be sanctioned by the Stewards of the National Steeplechase Association.

    (N. B. The National Steeplechase Association will not sanction meetings held by Country Clubs or Hunt Clubs)

    (II.) At any meeting advertised to take place *Number of* solely under these rules, there shall be in each *Steeplechases.* day's programme at least two Steeplechases, one of which must be three miles or upwards.

    (III.) There shall be no Steeplechase less than *Distances.* two miles, and no hurdle race less than one and one-half miles.

    (IV.) In all Steeplechase courses excepting for *Number, height* races exclusively for hunters there shall be at least *and description* five fences in every mile. There shall be a Water *of fences, water* *jump, etc.* Jump at least twelve feet wide and two feet deep, to be left open or guarded only by a perpendicular fence not exceeding two feet in height. There shall be in each course at least one ditch

five feet wide and two feet deep, which ditch
shall be guarded on the taking off side, by a
single rail and on the landing side there shall be
a fence three feet six inches in height, and if of
dead brushwood or gorse, two feet in width. The
minimum perpendicular height of any jump shall
be 3 feet, 6 inches.

(V.) In all Hurdle race courses there shall be not *Number of*
less than four flights of hurdles in the first mile, *Hurdles in*
with an additional flight of hurdles for every quarter *Hurdle Races.*
of a mile or part thereof beyond that distance, the
height of the hurdles being not less than three feet
six inches from the bottom of the lower bar to the
top of the upper bar.

(VI.) In Steeplechases and Hurdle Races exclus- *Races for*
ively for hunters, the distances, dimensions, *Hunters.*
number and character of fences, prescribed by the
National ● Hunt Association shall govern at all
meetings under these rules.

(VII.) The lowest weights in handicaps shall be: *Lowest Weights*
For Steeplechases, -   -   -   - 135 pounds. *in Handicaps.*
For Hurdle Races and races for
    Hunters on the flat, -   -   130 pounds.

PART IV.

POWERS OF THE STEWARDS OF THE NATIONAL STEEPLECHASE ASSOCIATION.

4.   (I.) The Stewards of the National Steeplechase *Authority to*
Association have power to license any meeting, to *License Meetings,*
be run under these rules ; to recognize or refuse to *to Investigate and*
recognize any meeting or meetings as they may see *Punish.*
fit ; to grant and withdraw licenses to jockeys ; to
prohibit any person from acting in any official
capacity in connection with a meeting ; to investigate any case which may appear to them to
require their interference (whether or not referred
to them by the Stewards of a meeting), and give a
final decision thereon ; they have power to impose
any fine not exceeding $250, and to warn any
person off all the courses where these rules are in
force.

(II.) The Stewards of the National Steeplechase *No Cognizance* Association take no cognizance of any disputes or *of Betting.* claims with respect to bets.

PART V.

STEWARDS FOR MEETINGS.

5. (I.) There shall be at least two Stewards for *Two Stewards.* every meeting.

(II) Each Steward may appoint a deputy at any *Deputy Stewards* time, or if there be but one Steward present, he *may be* shall, in case of necessity, appoint one or more *Appointed.* persons to act with him. If none of the Stewards are present the officers of the Association owning the course shall request two or more persons to act during the absence of the Stewards. In case of emergency, the Stewards may, during a meeting, appoint a substitute to fill any of the offices for that meeting only.

(III.) Every complaint against an official shall *Complaints in* be made to the Stewards in writing, signed by the *Writing.* complainant.

(IV.) The Stewards shall have full power to *Authority on* make (and if necessary to vary) all such arrange- *Race Courses.* ments for the conduct of the meeting as they see fit, and under special circumstances, to put off any race from day to day until a Sunday intervene.

(V.) The Stewards have control over, and they *Free Access.* and the Stewards of the National Steeplechase Association have free access to all stands, weighing rooms, enclosures, and other places in use for the purpose of racing.

(VI.) They shall have power to exclude from all *Who may be* places under their control : *excluded from Race Courses.*

(a.) Every person who is warned off the turf.

(b.) Every person whose name has been published in the unpaid forfeit list until the default is cleared.

(c.) Every person who has been reported as a defaulter, until it has been officially notified that his default is cleared.

(d.) Every person who has been declared by the turf authorities of, or by the Stewards of any recognized meeting in this or any other country, to have been guilty of any corrupt or fraudulent practices on the turf.

(VII.) They shall also have supervision over all *Over night* entries to over-night events and declarations to *Entries.* handicaps.

(VIII.) The Stewards have power to regulate and *Authority over* control the conduct of all officials and of all trainers, *all Employees.* jockeys, grooms and other persons attendant on horses.

(IX.) The Stewards have power to punish at their *Power to Punish.* discretion any person subject to their control with a fine not exceeding $200 00 and with suspension from acting or riding at the same meeting, and to report to the Stewards of the National Steeplechase Association should they consider any further action necessary.

(X.) The Stewards have power to determine all *Power to* questions arising in reference to racing at the *Investigate races.* meeting, subject to appeal under Part XXI, and should no decision have been arrived at by the Stewards within seven days of the objection being lodged, the Clerk of the Course shall then report the case to the Stewards of the National Steeplechase Association, who may at their discretion decide the matter, and if they consider there has been negligence, may order any additional expense arising therefrom to be defrayed out of the funds of the meeting at which the case occurred.

(XI.) The Stewards have power to call for proof *Power to call for* that a horse is neither itself disqualified in any *Proof, etc.* respect, or nominated by, or the property, wholly or in part, of a disqualified person, and in default of such proof being given to their satisfaction, they may declare the horse disqualified.

(XII.) The Stewards have power at any time to *May make* order an examination by such person or persons *Examinations* as they think fit, of any horse entered for a race, or which has run in a race.

(XIII.) The Stewards as such, shall not enter- *Nothing to do* tain any disputes relating to bets. *with Bets.*

PART VI.

OFFICIALS OF MEETINGS.

6. An Inspector of the Steeplechase Courses shall *Inspector of* be annually appointed by, and will receive his *Steeplechase* instructions from the Stewards of the National *Courses.* Steeplechase Association.

7. The following officials shall be appointed for *Named Officials.* every meeting, subject to the approval of the Stewards, viz: Handicapper, Clerk of the Course, Clerk of the Scales, Forfeit Clerk, Starter, and one or more Judges. One person may, however, be appointed to fill two or more offices under this rule.

8. In all applications for licenses for meetings, the *Names of* names of all persons who are to act as officials of *Officials must be* the meeting must be given. *given.*

9. In case of emergency, the Stewards may, during *Substitutes may* a meeting, appoint a substitute to fill any of the *be appointed.* above named offices for that meeting only.

10. The Clerk of the Course or his deputy shall *Clerk of the* attend the Judges during each race ; he shall *Course.* discharge all the duties whether expressed or implied, required by the rules of racing, and report to the Stewards all violations of the rules of Racing or of the Regulations of the Course coming under his notice ; he shall keep a complete record of all races ; he shall receive all stakes, forfeits, entrance money, fines, arrears, purchase money in selling races, and pay over all the money collected by him to the Treasurer.

11. The Handicapper shall append to the weights for *Handicapper.* every handicap, the day and hour from which winners will be liable to a penalty, and no alteration shall be made after publication.

12. (1.) · The Clerk of the Scales shall exhibit the *Clerk of the* number (as allotted on the official card) of each *Scales.* horse for which a jockey has been weighed out, and shall forthwith furnish the Starter with a list of such numbers, and the numbers shall not be taken down until the horses are started.

(II.) If extra or special weight be declared for any horse, such weight shall be exhibited on the

Notice Board ; also any declaration to win, or
alteration of colors.

(III.) He shall in all cases weigh in the riders
of the horses and report to the Stewards any jockey
not presenting himself to be weighed in.

(IV.) The Clerk of the Scales shall always put
2 lbs. extra into the scales to prove that the horse
has not carried too much weight.

(V.) He shall at the close of each day's racing
send a return to the office of the Secretary of the
National Steeplechase Association, of the weights
carried in every race, and the names of the jockeys,
specifying overweight,.if any.

13. (I) The Starter shall give all orders necessary *Starter.*
for securing a fair start.

(II.) He shall report to the Stewards all cases of
misconduct by jockeys when under his orders.

(III.) He shall report to the Stewards the time at
which each race was actually started ; also the
time of the first, if any, false starts, which shall be
held to fix the time of starting for that race.   H e
shall also report by whom, or by what cause any
delay was occasioned.

14. (I.) The Judge or Judges must occupy the *Judges.*
Judges' box at the time the horses pass the winning
post, and their sole duty shall be to place the horses.
They must announce their decisions immediately,
and such decisions shall be final unless an objection to the winner or any placed horse is made and
sustained.   Provided, that this rule shall not prevent the Judges from correcting any mistake, such
correction being subject to confirmation by the
Stewards.

(II.) The Judge or Judges shall, at the close of
each day's racing, sign and send a report of the
result of each race to the office of the Secretary
of the National Steeplechase Association.

15. The Forfeit Clerk shall be in attendanae on *Forfeit Clerk.*
every race day of each meeting for the purpose of
enforcing the forfeit list, and for collecting forfeits
due.

PART VII.
OMITTED CONDITIONS.

16.   (I.) When the weights are omitted from the *Omission of Weights.* conditions of any race, the horses shall carry weight for age, subject to penalties and allowances.

(II.) When a scale of weights for age is not fixed *Weights to be carried.* by the regulations of any course, or by the conditions of a meeting or race, the following scale shall govern : FOR STEEPLECHASES

3 year olds	-	-	-	138 pounds.
4 " "	-	-	-	150 "
5 " "	-	-	-	162 "
6 " " and aged	-	. 172	"	

FOR HURDLE RACES AND RACES ON THE FLAT.

3 year olds	-	-	-	140 pounds.
4 " "	-	-	-	155 "
5 " "	-	-	-	165 "
6 " " and aged	-	168	"	

Except in handicaps and in races where the weights are fixed absolutely in the conditions, mares three years old and upwards shall be allowed 5 lbs. before the 1st of September and 3 lbs. afterwards. Geldings shall be allowed 3 lbs.

(III.) For other races on the flat the scale of weights adopted by the Jockey Club shall govern, and in respect of such races welter weights shall be twenty-eight pounds above the weights for age.

17.   (I.) When no course is mentioned, it shall be *Omission of Distance.* as follows :

If three years old, two miles.
If four years old, two miles and a half.
If five years old, three miles.
If six years old or upwards, four miles.

And if the horses be of different age, the course shall be fixed by the age of the youngest.

(II.) When no day is fixed for a race, it shall *If no day named.* be run on the last day of the meeting, unless otherwise agreed by all the parties engaged, and sanctioned by the Stewards.

PART VIII.
RACE HORSES.

18.   All horses entered for races to be run under *Registration of horses.* these rules must, for purposes of identification, be registered in the Registry Office. Applications

for registry must be accompanied by a certificate clearly establishing the identity of the horse and giving the name, if any, sex, age, color, marks and pedigree if known. The registry fee is $2.00 for each horse.

19.   If a horse entered for a race has not been registered prior to the day upon which the race is to be run, the Clerk of the Course may issue, upon the payment of a fee of $25, to go to the Registry Office, a temporary certificate of registry permitting the horse to start on that day only, provided the horse has been properly entered and his identity is satisfactorily established. *Horses may obtain temporary certificate.*

20.   If a horse that has been properly entered, but has not been registered, start in a race, he shall not, on that account, be disqualified, but his owner shall be fined $100, to be paid to the Registry Office. N. B —Horses registered in the Registry Office of the Jockey Club, or of the National Hunt Association, shall be deemed to be registered. *Horses not disqualified.*

21.   No horse shall run for a Steeplechase, or a Hurdle Race, until September 1st of the year in which he is three years old. *When three-year-olds may run.*

22.   Horses must be named before they run the second time. *Horses must be named.*

23.   Whenever the name under which a horse has run at a recognized meeting in any country is changed, the old name, as well as the new name, must be given until he has run three times over the course of a recognized association, and if he first runs under the new name in a race at a meeting held under these rules, the change of name must be notified to the Registry Office. *Changing names.*

24.   (I.) Every person subscribing to a sweepstake or entering a horse in a race to be run under these rules accepts the decision of the Stewards on any question relating to a race or to racing. *Decision of Stewards must be accepted.*

   (II.) At the discretion of the Stewards of the National Steeplechase Association or of the Stewards, and without notice, the entries of any person or the *transfer of any entry* may be refused.

25.   A horse is not qualified to run for any race unless he is duly entered for the same. *Horses must be duly entered*

26.   No horse is qualified to be entered or run which *Disqualified* is wholly or partly the property of, or in any way *persons cannot* under the care or superintendence of a disqualified *enter or run horses.* person.

27.   Any horse which has been the subject of fraud- *Fraudulent* ulent practice may be disqualified for such time *practices may* and for such races as the Stewards shall determine. *disqualify.*

28.   (I.) Joint subscriptions or entries may be made *Joint* by two or more owners in their individual names, *subscriptions and* or in the name of a partnership duly registered. *entries.*

(II.) If any of the parties to a joint subscription or entry die, its rights and liabilities remain in the survivor or survivors, subject to filing with the Secretary of the Stewards of the National Steeple-chase Association any change of interest in the engagement.

29.   The list of entries shall be closed at the adver- *Entries to close* tised time, and no entry shall be admitted on any *at advertised* ground after that time. In default of observance *time.* of this rule, the receiver of nominations shall be reported to the Stewards, and unless the nom-inator can prove to their satisfaction that the entry was made in due time, it shall be void.

PART IX.

ENTRIES, PARTNERSHIPS, ASSUMED NAMES.

30.   (I.) Entries and declarations of forfeit shall be *Entries and* made in writing, signed by the owner of the horse *Declarations in* or of the engagement, or by some person deputed *Writing.* by him.

(II.) Entries and declarations made by telegraph *May be* shall be equally binding. *telegraphed.*

(III) Entries to all races must be published, *Entries must* excepting entries f r over-night events. *be published.*

31.   (I.) An entry shall state the name or assumed *What Entries* name of the owner, the name, or description of the *shall State.* horse if unnamed, and if the race be for horses of different ages, the age of the horse entered.

(II) In entering a horse for the first time, it *Full description* shall be identified by stating its name (if it has *of horse in first* any), its color (when possible), whether a horse *entry.*

mare or gelding, and the names or description of its
sire and dam. If the dam was covered by more than
one stallion, the names or description of all must
be stated. In all cases such pedigree or description must be given as will clearly distinguish the
horse entered from all other horses; and if the
pedigree of the sire and dam is unknown, the
Stewards may at any time require in confirmation
of the entry such further particulars as to where,
when and from whom it was purchased or
obtained, as will identify it.

(III.) This description of the horse must be *When description*
repeated in every entry until a description of him *may be omitted.*
has been published in the programme or list of
entries of a recognized Association.

(IV.) In any entry after such publication his
name and age will be sufficient.

(V.) If a horse be entered with a name for the
first time in several races closing at the same place
on the same day, the description need not be given
in more than one of such entries.

32.   (I.) All partnerships must be registered annually *Partnerships*
with the National Steeplechase Association. *must be registered*
(II.) All partnerships and the names and ad- *ond published in*
dresses of every person having any interest in a *Racing Calendar*
horse, the relative proportions of such interest, and
the terms of any sale with contingencies, or of any
lease or arrangements, must be registered at least
half an hour previous to the race, with the Secretary of the National Steeplechase Association, or
with the Clerk of the Course, for transmission to
the Secretary of the Stewards of the National
Steeplechase Association, before a horse sold with
contingencies, or leased, or which is a joint property. can start for any race; and all partners shall
be jointly and severally liable for every stake or
forfeit.

(I.I.) All statements of partnership, sales with *To whom*
contingencies, leases or arrangements, shall declear *winnings shall be*
to whom winnings are payable and with whom the *payable,*
power of entry or declaration of forfeit rests, and
shall be filed and posted in the office of the Secre-

tary of the Stewards of the National Steeplechase Association and published in the Racing
Calendar, but the real names of persons who have
registered assumed names shall not be disclosed.
The signature of each party to a partnership is
required.

33.   (I.) An owner or partnership of owners may *Assumed Names.*
assume a name which must be filed with the Sec-
retary of the Stewards of the National Steeplechase
Association, and such assumed name must be so
filed at least twenty-four hours before the same is
used.

(II) An owner cannot have more than one
assumed name, nor can he use his real name in
any subscription or entries so long as he has an
assumed name registered.

(III.) An assumed name cannot be registered
which has been already registered, or is the real
name of any owner of race horses.

(IV.) An assumed name cannot be changed during the calendar year of its registration, but it may
be abandoned at any time and the real name or
names substituted in all entries or subscriptions.

PART X.

CONDITIONS OF ENTRY, ETC.

34.   (I.) In the event of a horse being entered for *Errors in entries*
a race with the wrong age, or an incorrect or im- *may be corrected*
perfect description according to the rules of racing, *on payment of*
the entry may be corrected on the payment of a fine *fine.*
of $10 for each entry, provided it be proved to the
satisfaction of the Stewards that the error was
accidental, and provided also that the correction
be made before the numbers are exhibited for
that race, and provided further that error as to age
be corrected before the weights for a handicap in
which the horse is engaged are announced.

(II.) On the payment of the fine the entry of a
horse may within a like time be omitted from a
race for which it was not qualified, e. g. a colt for
a filly stakes, but no horse may be substituted.

(III.) The fines under this rule to go to the winner, unless the winner be the person fined, when his fine shall go to the second horse.

(IV.) When an hour for closing is stated, entries or declarations of forfeit for sweepstakes cannot be received afterwards. *Entries or Declarations, when and where made.*

(V.) If the hour is not stated, they may be mailed or telegraphed up to midnight of the day of closing, but if miscarriage is alleged, satisfactory proof of the mailing or telegraphing must be presented within reasonable time, or the entry or declaration of forfeit shall not be received.

(VI) In the absence of notice to the contrary, entries and declarations of forfeit happening on the eve of and during a race meeting, close at the office of the Clerk of the Course at the Course.

(VII.) A person who subscribes to a sweepstake before the time fixed for naming, can transfer the right of entry under one or more of his subscriptions. *Subscriptions Transferable.*

(VIII.) An entry of a horse in a sweepstake is a subscription to the sweepstake. A subscription cannot be withdrawn, but before the time of closing an entry of a horse in any race may be corrected or another horse may be substituted. *Subscriptions cannot be withdrawn, but may be corrected.*

(IX.) Supscriptions and all entries or rights of entry under them become void on the death of the subscriber, except when a horse is sold with the engagement and transfer by the subscriber, and acknowledgment of liability by the purchaser, both in writing, have been delivered to the Clerk of the Course previous to the death of the subscriber, or, except when entries under his subscription have been previously made by the transferee of a right of entry. *Subscription void if nominator dies.*

(X.) If either party to a match die, the match is off.

35. (I.) No horse shall be considered as struck out of any of his engagements until the owner or some duly authorized person shall have given notice in writing, or by telegraph to the Clerk of the Course where the horse is engaged. *Declarations and striking out of Engagements.*

(II.) The day and hour of its receipt shall be recorded and early publicity given thereto.

. (III). The striking of a horse out of an engagement is irrevocable.

(IV.) Omission to strike a horse out of an engagement, not sold or transferred with him, does not entitle his owner to start him, or to the stakes if he wins.

(V.) The notification of the death of a horse shall be equivalent to a declaration of forfeit.

(VI.) When a horse is sold with his engagements, *Sales with* or any part of them, the seller cannot strike the *Engagements.* horse out of any such engagements, but, on default of the purchaser, remains liable for the amount of forfeit in each.

(VII) In all cases of sale by private treaty, the *Proof of transfer* written acknowledgement of both parties that the *of engagements* horse was sold with engagements is necessary to *must be filed.* prove the fact, but when the horse is sold by public auction or claimed out of a selling race, the advertised conditions of either sale or race are sufficient evidence.

(VIII.) If certain engagements only be speci- *Only* fied, those only are sold with the horse. *Engagements specified sold.*

PART XI.

ENTRANCE MONEY, FORFEITS, STAKES, ETC.

36.   (I.) Entries for purses, in the absence of condi- *Entries for* tion or notice to the contrary, are to be made at the *purses, when made.* office of the Clerk of the Course, at the course, by 4 o'clock P. M., of the day previous to the race, or, if there be races at the course that day, within thirty minutes after the last race.

(II.) No entry for a purse shall be received after the time for closing.

(III.) Entrance money for a purse is not *Entrance money* returned on the death of a horse or his failure to *not returnable.* start for any cause whatever.

(IV.) Entries in purses are not void on the *Entries in purses* death of the nominator, *not void by death*

(V.) Entrance money, forfeits, stakes and arrears *Entrances and* must be paid in cash (if so required), to the Clerk *forfeits to be paid in cash.* of the Course, and entrance money must be paid *in cash.* at the time of entry, except entrance money for free handicap purses.

37. (I.) The nominator is liable, as well as every *All persons* partner in the horse, at the time of nomination, and *owning interests* also any purchaser of the horse whose acceptance of *in horse, liable.* the engagement has been lodged with the Clerk of the Course and accepted by the Stewards of the National Steeplechase Association, for the entrance money and stake or forfeit.

(II.) A person making a wrong nomination is equally liable.

(III.) Every horse will be considered as having *Owner liable* started and be liable for whatever is due for so *after Jockey* doing, when its jockey has been weighed and its *weighs.* number displayed.

(IV.) A subscriber to a sweepstakes is liable for *If transferee* the stake or forfeit, but if he transfer the right of *don't pay,* entry to any other person he is liable only in *subscriber liable.* case of default by the transferee.

(V.) A person making an entry under another per- *When subscriber* son's subscription where forfeit must be declared *not Liable.* by a particular time, shall, if he does not declare forfeit by that time, be considered to have taken the engagement upon himself, and it shall be transferred to his name.

(VI.) A jockey shall not be weighed out for any *Stakes, Entrance* race unless there shall have been previously paid : *Money and*
(a.) Any stake, forfeit or entrance money *Arrears must be* payable by the owner or nominator in respect to *weighing out.* that race.
(b.) All arrears due from any person for such horse, or due for the same or any other horse from any person by whom such horse is wholly or partly owned, or in whose name or under whose subscription he is entered,

PART XII.

THE UNPAID FORFEIT LIST.

38. (I.) An unpaid Forfeit List shall be kept at the *Forfeit List to be* Registry Office, and may be published in the *published.*

Calendar on the first days of January, April, July
and October. It shall include all arrears which
shall have been notified by the Clerk of the Course
of any meeting held under these rules, or by the
Registry Office of the Jockey Club or the National
Hunt Association, and by any turf authority having reciprocal arrangements with the National
Steeplechase Association for the mutual enforcement of forfeits.

(II.) Where a person is prevented by these rules *Arrears paid to*
from entering or starting a horse for any race *qualify horse*
without paying arrears, for which he would not *may be put in*
otherwise be liable, he may, by paying the same, *Forfeit List.*
enter or start the horse and place the arrears
on the Forfeit List as due to himself, and in like
manner, the seller of a horse with engagements
may, if compelled to pay them by the purchaser's
default, place the amount on the Forfeit List as
due from the purchaser to himself.

(III.) So long as the name of a person is in the *Disabilities of*
Forfeit List no horse which has been entered by *persons and*
him, or in his name, or under his subscription, or *horses in unpaid*
of which he is or was at the time of entry, wholly *Forfeit List.*
or partly the owner, can run for any race, and no
horse which shall be proved to the satisfaction of
the Stewards to be directly or indirectly under the
care, training, management, or superintendence
of a person whose default has been twice published
in the Racing Calendar, shall be qualified to be
entered or run for any race. So long as any horse
is in the Forfeit List, such horse shall not be
qualified to be run for any race.

(IV.) The entry of a horse which, or the owner of *Persons*
which, is in the Forfeit List, shall not be accepted, *nominating*
and any person nominating a horse in contraven- *horses in Forfeit*
tion of these rules may be fined $100. *List may be fined*

PART XIII.

QUALIFICATION OF STARTERS.   *Starters must be*

39.   (I.) A horse shall not be qualified to run in a race *named 30*
unless he has been announced as a starter and *minutes before*
race.

the name of his jockey given to the Clerk of the Course or the Clerk of the Scales not less than 30 minutes before the time appointed for the race, which shall, at the close of the previous race of the day, be indicated on a dial conspicuously placed.

(II) Any subsequent change of jockey must be sanctioned by the Stewards, and if satisfactory reason is not given for the change, they may fine, suspend or rule off the course any person they think culpable in the matter. *Sanction of Stewards necessary to change jockey.*

(III) If the race be one for which the entry was made during the meeting, a horse must start unless struck out 30 minutes before the time appointed for the race. *Horses must start if not struck out 30 minutes before race.*

(IV.) In all races, should a horse become disabled after weighing out, if so proven to the satisfaction of the Stewards, he may be withdrawn. *Horses disabled may withdraw.*

(V.) If the time for the first race is not fixed by the programme, it shall be indicated on the dial half an hour in advance. *When time not fixed for first race.*

PART XIV.
ESTIMATED WINNINGS.

40.   (I.) The value of prizes not in money must be advertised. *Value of races, how calculated. What shall be deducted, and in case of walk-over*

(II.) Prizes, stakes and forfeits in a race belong to the winner, except as otherwise declared in the conditions.

(III.) In estimating the value of the race, there shall be deducted the amount of the winner's own stake, and any money payable to other horses, or out of the stakes by the conditions of the race, or by the general conditions of the meeting, entrance money to a purse, or entrance money going to the race fund shall not be deducted.

(IV.) No plate or sweepstake shall be run for, unless the clear value to the winner, calculated as above, in case the race be run by two or more horses, will amount to $150, but if the value would amount to $150 if the race were so run, a horse may walk over, although he thereby receives less than $150.

(V.) In all sweepstakes (private sweepstakes excepted) or purses, the second horse shall at least save his entrance.

(VI.) When a cup other than a challenge cup is advertised to be run for, it shall be given even in the event of a walk over.

(VII.) When a walk-over (except after a dead-heat) is the result of an arrangement by the owners of horses engaged, neither a cup or any portion of the advertised money need be given.

(VIII.) In case of a walk-over (except after a dead-heat) one-half the money offered to the winner is given.

41.   (I.) In estimating the amount a horse has won *Winnings, how* in any one or more races, account shall be taken of *calculated.* cups or moneys, whether derived from stakes, bonus or any source, gained by him in Steeple-chases, hurdle races or hunter races on the flat, in any country. of the value of $150 and upwards.

(II.) Winnings during the year shall include all prizes from the 1st of January preceding to the time appointed for the start, winnings shall include dividings, walking over or receiving forfeit.

(III.) Winning of a fixed sum is understood to be winning it in one race, unless specified to the contrary.

(IV.) A Challenge Cup is not estimated in the *Value of* value of a race until it is finally won, provided the *Challenge Cup* sweepstakes or added money amount to $150 or *not calculated till* upwards, but when won out-right the winner must *won.* carry a penalty in respect to the full value of the Cup and money prize.

42.   Any money or prize which by the conditions is *Distribution of* to go to the horse placed second, or in any lower *second or third* place in the race, shall, if the winner have walked *Money in case of* over, or no horse has been so placed, be dealt with *Walkover or no* *Horse placed.* as follows :

(a.) If part of the stake, it shall go to the winner ; or

(b.) If a separate donation from the race fund or any other source, it shall not be given at all ; or

(c.) If entrance money for the race, it shall go to the race fund.

43.   (I.) If a race never be run, or be void, stakes, *Money returned* forfeits and entrance money shall be returned. *if race void.*

(II.) A race shall be declared void if no qualified *When horses shall* horse cover the course a·cording to rule, and *not be placed.* within thirty minutes after the start, and no horse finishing five minutes or more behind the winner shall be placed.

PART XV.

PENALTIES, ALLOWANCES AND WEIGHING.

44.   (I.) When a race is in dispute both the horse *Penalties.* that came in first and any horse claiming the race shall be liable to all the penalties attaching to the winner of that race, until the matter be decided.

(II.) No horse shall carry extra weight for having run second or in any lower place in a race.

(III.) Extra weight shall not be incurred in respect of private sweepstakes or matches, for steeplechases or hurdle races.

(IV.) When winners of selling races are exempted from penalties the exception does not apply to races in which any of the horses running are not to be sold.

(V.) Penalties and allowances are not cumulative, unless so declared by the conditions of the race.

45.   (I.) Allowances must be claimed at the time of *Allowances must* entry when practicable, but omission to claim is *be claimed.* not a source of disqualification, and a claim for allowance to which a horse is not entitled does not disqualify, unless carried out at scale.

(II.) Allowances to the produce of untried *In Produce* horses are for the produce of horses whose pro-*Races.* duce never won a race in any country.

(III.) No horse shall receive allowance of weight *No beaten* or be relieved from extra weight for having been *Allowances.* beaten in one or more races. provided that this rule shall not prohibit maiden allowances or allowances to horses that have not won within a specified time or races of a specified value.

46.   (I.) Every jockey must be weighed for a specified *Weighing out.* horse not less than 20 minutes before the time fixed for the race, and the number of the horse shall be exhibited officially as soon as possible.

(II.) If a horse run in a hood, muzzle, martingale, breast-plate or clothing, it must be put on the scale and included in the jockey's weight.

(III.) No whip or substitute for a whip shall be allowed on the scales, nor shall any bridle be weighed.

47.   (I.) If a jockey intend to carry more than 2 lbs. *Overweight.* over-weight, he must declare the amount thereof at the time of weighing out, or, if in doubt, as to his proper weight, he may declare the weight he intends to carry.

(II.) A horse shall not be qualified to run in a *May carry more* race with more than 5 lbs. overweight except *than 5 Pounds* in races confined to gentlemen and qualified riders *Overweight.* and when permitted by the conditions of the race or meeting.

(III.) The owner or his representative is re- *Owner's* sponsible for the weight his horse carries. *Responsibility.*

(IV.) Any over weight, or any change of weight *Overweight, or* from the weight stated in the official programme, *Change of* it is to be immediately posted on the Notice Board. *Weight on Notice Board.*

PART XVI.

STARTING.

48.   If a horse whose number has been exhibited, or *Explanations* whose starting is obligatory, does not start and *Required of* run the race, the Stewards may call on the owner, *Failure to Run.* trainer or jockey for an explanation, and if no satisfactory explanation is given, shall fine, sus· pend or rule off the course, as the case may warrant.

49.   After the horses are ordered to the starting post, *Only Officials on* and until the Stewards direct the gates to be re- *Course during* opened, all persons except the racing officials shall *race.* be excluded from the course to be run over.

50.   (I.) A bell will be rung ten minutes and a bugle *Signals for the* *Start.*
sounded five minutes before the time fixed for the
start.

(II.) The trainer or jockey of a horse not at the *Trainer or* *Jockey to be* *Fined if Late.*
post, ready to start, at the appointed time, shall be
fined.

51.   (I.) The position of horses when starting shall *Positions of* *Horses in* *Starting.*
be determined by lot, i. e., a numbered ball shall
be drawn from a bottle by the Clerk of the Scales
when the jockeys weigh out.

(II.) Nevertheless, the starter may place vicious *Vicious or* *Unruly Horses* *may be Placed* *Behind the Line.*
or unruly horses where they cannot injure others,
by placing them behind the line in the position
which they have drawn.

52.   (I.) A horse in the hands of the starter shall *Horses in* *Starters' Hands.*
receive no further care from his attendants.

(II.) With the sanction of the starter. a horse *Horses may be* *led into Position.*
may be led to his position, but must then be
released to his jockey. The jockey must not dismount, except to set right insecure equipments,
and then only with the permission of the starter.

(III.) If an accident happen to a jockey or his *Jockeys may* *Dismount by per-* *mission of* *Starter.*
equipments, the starter may allow the other
jockeys to dismount and their horses to be cared
for, unless the delay is likely to be of short
duration.

53.   (I.) A start in front of the post is void, and the *The Start.*
horse must be started again.

(II.) The horses shall be started by a flag, and *No recall after* *advance flag* *dropped.*
there shall be no start until, and no recall after, the
assistant starter has dropped his flag in answer to
the flag of the starter.

(III.) The starter shall give all orders necessary
for securing a fair start.

(IV.) The horses shall be started as far as *May be Started a* *reasonable dis-* *tance back of* *Post.*
possible in a line, but may be started at such
reasonable distance behind the starting post as
the starter thinks necessary.

(V.) Any jockey misconducting himself at the *Jockeys may be* *punished for* *misbehavior.*
post, refusing to obey the commands of the starter
in any respect whatever, wilfully turning his horse
round, hanging behind, not starting when the flag

is dropped, or otherwise attempting to take any advantage, shall be reported to the Stewards. The suspension of a jockey for misbehavior at the post shall not take effect until after the last race of the day of his sentence.

(VI.) The concurrent statement of the starter and his assistant as to incidents of the start is conclusive. *Concurrent Statements.*

PART XVII.

RUNNING AND WALKING OVER.

54.   An owner running two or more horses in a race may declare to win with one of them, and such declaration must be made at the time of weighing out, and is to be immediately posted on the Notice Board. A jockey riding a horse with which his owner has not declared to win, must on no account stop such horse except in favor of the stable companion on whose behalf declaration to win has been made. *Declaration to Win.*

55.   (I.) In a flag race a leading horse is entitled to any part of the course, but when there is a clear opening to pass him, he shall not impede another horse by crossing so as to compel him to shorten his stride. *May disqualify for crossing, jostling, foul riding, running out of the course, carrying short weight, etc.*

(II.) In a Steeplechase or Hurdle Race, a horse shall be disqualified if his rider, by foul riding, jeopardized the chances of success of any other horse in a race, and in the run home from the last hurdle or fence, a horse which crosses another is disqualified, unless it be proved that he was two clear lengths ahead of the other horses when he crossed. The Stewards have power to fine a rider for the above offense any sum not exceeding $2ö0. In all cases the Stewards have power of suspending a rider until the expiration of the meeting, or should they consider such punishment insufficient, until the case can be heard and decided by the Stewards of the National Steeplechase Association.

(III.) If a horse or his rider jostles another horse or rider, the aggressor is disqualified, unless it be proved that the jostle was wholly caused by the fault of some other rider. or that the jostled horse or his rider was partially in fault.

(IV.) If a horse run the wrong side of a post, he must turn back and run the course from such post.

(V.) If a jockey wilfully strike another horse or jockey, or ride wilfully or carelessly so as to injure another horse, which is in no way in fault, or so as to cause another horse to do so, his horse is disqualified.

(VI.) When a horse is disqualified under this rule, or for being short of weight, every horse in the race belonging wholly or partially to the same owner, is also disqualified.

(VII.) Complaints under this rule can only be received from the owner, trainer or jockey of the horse alleged to be aggrieved, and must be made to the Clerk of the Scales, or to the Stewards, before, or immediately after, his jockey has passed the scales. But nothing in this rule shall prevent the Stewards from taking cognizance of foul riding. *Complaints only received from Owner, Trainer or Jockey.*

(VIII.) A jockey whose horse has been disqualified or who unnecessarily causes his horse to shorten his stride, with a view to complaint, or an owner, trainer or jockey who complains frivilously that his horse was crossed or jostled, may be fined or suspended. *Jockeys may be fined or suspended.*

56.   If the Stewards at any time are satisfied that the riding of any race was intentionally foul, or that the jockey was instructed or induced so to ride, all persons guilty of complicity in the offense shall be ruled off. *Intentional foul riding.*

57.   If a horse leave the course he must turn back and run the course from the point at which he left it. *Horse-bolting.*

58.   If a race has been run by all the horses at wrong weights, or over a wrong course or distance, or if a judge is not in the stand when the horses pass the winning post, the race shall be run again after the last race of the day, but at an interval of not less than twenty minutes if for two miles or less, or than thirty minutes if over two miles. *When a race is to be run again.*

59.   A walk over shall in no case be deemed neces- *Walking over* sary. It shall be sufficient if a horse be weighed *not necessary.* out for mounted and proceed to the starting post, when if no competitor appear in due time, he shall be considered the winner.

PART XVIII.

WEIGHING IN.

60.   (I.) Every jockey must immediately after *Every Jockey* pulling up ride his horse to the place of weighing, *must return* dismount after obtaining permission of the Judge, *promptly to the* and present himself to be weighed by the Clerk of *scales.* the Scales ; provided that if a jockey be prevented from riding to the place of weighing by reason of accident or illness by which he or his horse is disabled, he may walk or be carried to the scales.

(II.) Every jockey must upon pulling up *Jockeys must un-* unsaddle his own horse, and no attendant shall *saddle their* touch the horse, except by the bridle. *horses.*

(III.) If a jockey does not present himself to *Horses to be dis-* weigh in, or be one pound short of his proper or *qualified if one* declared weight, or be guilty of any fraudulent *pound short of* practice with respect to weight or weighing, his *weight.* horse is disqualified. If a jockey dismount before reaching the scales, or touch (except accidentally), any person or thing other than his own equipments before weighing in, his horse is disqualified, unless he can satisfy the Stewards that he was justified by extraordinary circumstances.

(IV.) A jockey omitting to obtain permission *Jockeys omitting* to dismount or disregarding any requirement as *to obtain permis-* to weight or weighing, shall be fined or suspended, *sion to dismount.* and may be ruled off the course.

(V.) If a horse carry more than two pounds over *Horses may be* his proper or declared weight, he is disqualified, *disqualified if* unless the Stewards be satisfied that such excess *more than two* of weight has been caused by wet or mud. *pounds over-weight.*

PART XIX.

DEAD HEATS.

61.   (I) In races on the flat, a dead heat for the *When run off, if* first place, is to be run off on the same day, at the *no division.*

time the Stewards appoint, but at an interval of
not less than twenty minutes, unless the race
admits of division and the owners agree to divide,
or one of the horses making such a dead heat be
withdrawn.

(II.) The other horses shall be deemed to have *Other Horses,*
been beaten, but they shall be entitled to their *how placed.*
place (if any) as if the race had been finally determined the first time.

(III.) If in running a dead heat off, either horse *In case of a foul*
should be disqualified, it shall be decided by the *in running off.*
Stewards whether the disqualification shall extend
to the loss of the second place, and, if so, the
horse that originally ran third shall be entitled to
the second place.

62.   When a dead heat is run for second place, and *Dead heats for*
an objection is made to the winner of the race, if *second place when*
such objection be declared valid in time for the *winner objected*
dead heat to be run off on the day of the race, *to.*
the Stewards may direct it to be run off accord-
ingly ; otherwise the horses which run the dead
heat shall divide.

63.   ·If a dead heat be run by two or more horses for *Dead heats for*
second or any lower place in a race, the owners *second or lower*
shall divide, subject to the provisions of the last *place.*
preceding rule.

64.   In races on the flat, every horse running a dead *Horses running*
heat for first place, shall be deemed the winner of *a dead heat*
the race until the dead heat is determined, or the *deemed winners if*
owners agree to divide, and if the owners agree to *owners divide.*
divide, each horse which divides. shall be deemed
a winner of the race. and be liable to any penalty
for the full amount he would have received if he
had won.

65.   Every horse running a dead heat for second *Dead heat for*
or a lower place shall be liable to any penalty or *second or lower*
disability attaching to the place. *place may be*
penalized.

DEAD HEATS.   STEEPLECHASE OR HURDLE RACES.

In Steeplechase or Hurdle Races a dead heat *Dead heats for*
66.   shall not be run over, but the money shall be *steeplechase or*
hurdle race shall
divided.   In such an event the horses so dividing *not be run off.*
shall only be considered to have won their share
of the money.

67.   When owners divide they shall divide equally *Division to be*
all the moneys and other prizes which any of *equal in all cases*
them could take, if the dead heat were run off.

68.   If the dividing owners cannot agree as to which *When owners can-*
of them is to have a cup or other prize which can *not agree on*
not be divided, the question shall be determined *division.*
by lot by the Stewards, who shall decide what
sum of money shall be paid by the owner who
takes such cup, or other individual prize, to the
other owner or owners.

69.   On a dead heat for a match, the match is off.   *Match off if*
dead heat.

PART XX.

SELLING RACES.

70.   In selling races which close within 48 hours of *Can only start*
the race day, no owner shall start more than one *one Horse.*
horse.

71.   The winner of every selling race must be sold *Winner to be*
at auction, (unless entered not to be sold, under *sold.*
the conditions of the race.)

72.   (I.) Every horse running in a selling race, except *Disposal of sur-*
the winner, is liable to be claimed for the selling *plus after*
price plus the value of the purse or stake by *auction sale.*
the owner of any other horse running in the
race. The sale of the winner shall take place
immediately after the race, and the surplus over
the selling price shall go one half to the second
horse and the other half to the race fund, or the
whole to the race fund if no second or third horse
be placed.

(II.) Every horse running a dead heat for first *How Horses run-*
place in a selling steeplechase or hurdle race shall be *ning dead heats*
sold, but the price for which each horse is entered *in Steeplechases*
to be sold shall be increased by the difference *or Hurdle races*
between the value of the purse or stakes actually *shall be sold.*
won and the value of the purse or stakes that would
have gone to the winner if the race had been won
outright by one horse. The surplus, if any, over
the amount for which each horse is sold and the
selling price (increased as above provided), shall
go to the race fund.

(III.) If sold or bought in, the horse shall not *Horses not paid for may be sold again.* leave the place of sale without permission of the Clerk of the Course, and if the horse be not paid for within 15 minutes. or the price secured to his satisfaction, he may direct the horse to be put up a second time, and the purchaser at the first sale shall be responsible for any deficiency arising from the second, and shall be treated as a defaulter until it is paid.

73.
(I.) Owners of horses placed shall have priority *All Horses other than the winner may be claimed.* of claim in the order of the places, and if the owners of two or more horses having equal rights claim, they are to draw lots. The owner of the winner has the last claim.

(II.) No person can claim more than one horse. *Can only claim one.*

(III.) Every claim must be made in writing to the *How and when claimed.* Clerk of the Course or the Clerk of the Scales not later than a quarter of an hour after the winner has passed the scales, and must be accompanied by the purchase money if required.

(IV.) The price of every horse claimed must be *Must be paid to Clerk of Course.* paid to the Clerk of the Course and an order given by him for the delivery of the horse.

(V.) In the case of a horse being claimed, if the *If claimant defaults.* price be not paid within 15 minutes after the claim is made, the claimant forfeits his right : but the owner may insist on the claimant taking and paying for the horse, and if he refuse or neglect to do so, he shall be treated as a defaulter in respect of the price.

74.
If a horse walk over, or there be no second horse *Walk-over for Selling race.* placed for a selling race, the winner is still liable to be sold, but he shall receive all the money offered by the conditions of the race to the winner, and any surplus from the sale shall go to the race fund.

75.
The following special provisions apply to claim- *Special provisions for selling and claiming races.* ing and selling races :

(I.) In case of a dead heat for a race on the flat, the time for claiming or selling is postponed until the dead heat is run off.

(II.) If an objection to the winner of a selling race be not decided before the time for selling, the

horse objected to and the horse subsequently
adjudged to be the winner shall be put at auction,
and any surplus from the sale of either shall be
treated as surplus from the sale of the winner, but
liability to be sold shall end with the day of the race.

(III.) If an objection to a horse which has been
claimed be declared valid, the claimant may within
such a time as the Stewards consider reasonable,
reject or return the horse and place on the forfeit
list any default by the owner in repayment of the
price.

(IV.) Any person refusing to deliver a horse
bought or claimed in a selling race shall be ruled
off, and the horse shall be disqualified for all races.

(V.) Any person failing to pay for a horse bought
or claimed in a selling race may be ruled off.

(VI.) Any person who shall attempt to prevent
another person from bidding on the winner of a
selling race, or claiming any horse in such race,
or demand any portion of the surplus from the
owners of horses which are entitled to it, or any
owner running selling races who may make an
agreement for the protection of each others horses
in contravention of these rules shall be ruled off.

(VII.) In all cases of races with selling con- *Cannot sell or*
ditions in which horses may be entered, or may run *claim Horses en-*
not to be sold, only such horses as run to be sold, *tered not to be*
shall be liable to be sold or claimed, and with this *sold.*
exception the foregoing rules relating to selling
races shall apply.

PART XXI.

DISPUTES, OBJECTIONS, APPEALS, ETC.

76.   (I.) Every objection shall be decided by the *Objections shall*
Stewards, but their decisions shall be subject to *be decided by*
appeal to the Stewards of the National Steeplechase *the Stewards.*
Association, so far as relates to points involving the
interpretation of these rules, or to any question
other than a question of fact, on which there shall be
no appeal, unless by leave of the Stewards, and
with the consent of the Stewards of the National

Steeplechase Association. Notice of appeal must be given in writing to the Clerk of the Course within 48 hours of the decision being made known.

(II.) In deciding a question on appeal, the Stewards of the National Steeplechase Association may call in any member of the National Steeple-chase Association to their assistance. or may, if they think the importance or difficulty of the case require such a course, refer it to a general meeting. *Appeal may be referred to a general meeting.*

(I.) Every objection must be made by the owner, trainer or jockey of some horse engaged in the race, or by the officials of the course, to the Clerk of the Scales, or to one of the Stewards. *Objections by whom, when and how made.*

(II.) All objections must be put in writing and signed by the objector.

(III.) An objection cannot be withdrawn without leave of the Stewards

(IV.) The Judge or Judges or their authorized substitute must occupy the Judge's box, at the time the horses pass the winning post. The decision must be announced immediately. and such decision shall be final unless an objection to the winner or any placed horse or horses is made and sustained ; provided that this Rule shall not prevent the Judge from correcting any mistake, such correction being subject to confirmation by the Stewards. *Judges must occupy their box and make prompt decision.*

(V.) All costs and expenses in relation to determining an objection or conducting an inquiry shall be paid by such person or persons and in such proportions as the Stewards shall direct. *Cost and expenses of objection to be paid.*

(VI.) Before considering an objection, the Clerk of the Course or Stewards may require a deposit, which shall be forfeited if the objection is decided to be frivolous or vexatious. *May require a deposit*

VII.) If an objection to a horse engaged in a race be made not later than noon of the day of the race, the Stewards may require the qualification to be proved before the race, and in default of such proof being given to their satisfaction, they may declare the horse disqualified. *Objection may be made before a race.*

(VIII.) An objection to any decision of the *Objection to decision of Clerk of Scales.* Clerk of the Scales must be made at once.

(IX.) An objection to the distance of a course *Objection to distance of a course.* officially designated must be made before the race.

(X.) An objection to a horse on the ground *Objection to Horse having run wrong course.* of his not having run the proper course, or of the race having been run on a wrong course, or of any other matter occurring in the race (except those coming under Rule 75) must be made before the numbers of the horses placed in the race are put up, unless under special circumstances the Stewards are satisfied that it could not have been made within that time.

(XI.) An objection on the ground *General objections.*

(a.) Of mis-statement, omission or error in the entry under which a horse has run ; or

(b.) That the horse which ran was not the horse or of the age which he was represented to be at the time of entry ; or

(c.) That he was not qualified under the conditions of the race, or by reason of default, entered in the forfeit list ; or

(d.) That he has run in contravention of the rules of partnership or registration. (See Rules 32 and 33.) May be received up to forty-eight hours, exclusive of Sunday, after the last race of the last day of the meeting.

(XII.) In any other case an objection must be *Objections for alleged fraud.* made within forty-eight hours of the race being run, exclusive of Sunday, save in the case of any fraud, or wilful mis-statement when there shall be no limit to the time of objecting, provided, the Stewards are satisfied that there has been no unnecessary delay on the part of the objector.

(XIII.) If an objection to a horse which has *Effect of disqualification by objection.* won be declared valid, the horse shall be regarded as having been last.

N. B. (For qualification of this rule, see Rule 55.)

(XIV.) If by reason of an objection to a horse *Money may be Recovered.* a race or place is awarded to another, his owner

can recover the money for such race or place from
those who wrongfully received it, and in case of
default can place it in the forfeit list.

(XV.) Pending the determination of an objec- *Moneys may be*
tion, any prize which the horse objected to may *Retained.*
have won or may win in the race, or any money
held by the Clerk of the Course as the price of a
horse claimed or bought in a selling race, (if
affected by the determination of the objection)
shall be withheld until the objection is determined, and any forfeit payable by the owner of
any other horse shall be paid to. and held by the
Clerk of the Course for the person who may be
entitled to it.

PART XXII.

JOCKEYS' LICENSES.

78.   (I.)   Where meetings are held under these rules, *Jockeys must be*
no jockey will be allowed to ride in a Steeplechase *licensed.*
or Hurdle races unless he has received a license
from the Stewards of the National Steeplechase
Association, and no jockey will be allowed to
ride in Flat Races unless he has received a
license from the Stewards of the National Steeplechase Association or the Stewards of the Jockey
Club, and no gentleman rider or qualified rider
will be allowed to ride in any races unless he
has received a license from the National Hunt
Association.   The Stewards of the National
Steeplechase Association may suspend or withdraw
any license issued by them to a jockey, and may
forbid a jockey holding a license from The Jockey
Club or a gentleman rider or qualified rider holding a license from the National Hunt Association,
from riding in races at meetings held under these
rules.

(II.)   A license from the National Steeplechase *Licenses to be*
Association must be applied for annually, with *applied for*
the full name and address of the applicant. It *annually.*
may be revoked or suspended at any time by the
Stewards of the National Steeplechase Association.

(III) The fee for a jockey's license shall be $10. *License fee, $10.*

(IV) In cases of emergency the Stewards *May ride* may permit jockeys to ride pending action on *pending action.* their application.

(V.) Any person who shall employ a jockey *Effect of* in contravention of this rule, shall be liable to *violating rule.* be fined by the Stewards of the National Steeplechase Association.

(VI.) Boys never having ridden in a race may *Boys may ride* be allowed to ride twice before applying for a *twice before* license, and licenses shall not be granted to boys *license issue.* who have never ridden in a race.

(VII.) No jockey whose license has been with- *Effect of license* drawn or refused, will be eligible to ride trials *withdrawn.* or train horses, or be allowed the privileges of the course during such time.

79.   (I.) License will be granted only under the fol- *Jockeys shall not* lowing conditions : Jockeys shall not be owners or *be Owners.* part owners of any race horse.

(II.) Leave may be given under exceptional cir- *Leave to own* cumstances on special application, to jockeys to *horses may be* own one or more horses, but this permission will *granted.* only be granted by the Stewards of the National Steeplechase Association when a jockey is also a trainer and the horse is trained in his own stable.

80.   (I) Any jockey who shall be proved to the satis- *Jockeys must not* faction of the Stewards to have any interest in *Bet.* any race horse or to have been engaged in any betting transaction, or to have received presents from persons other than the owner, will have his license at once revoked

(II.) Any person knowingly acting in the capacity of part owner or trainer of any horse in which a jockey possesses any interest, or making any bet with or on behalf of any jockey, or otherwise aiding or abetting in any breach of the orders of the Stewards, will be ruled off.

81.   The term of all contracts between jockeys and *Jockeys* their employers shall be filed with the Stewards *Retainers.* of the National Steeplechase Association and must be approved by them before a license be ·

granted and such contracts shall contain a provision that in case a jockey's license be revoked or suspended, the salary of the jockey shall in the former case cease, and in the latter case during the time of his suspension.

82.   (I.) If a jockey engaged for a race, or for a specified time, refuse to fulfill his engagements, or if a jockey ride without the consent of his employer, the Stewards may fine or suspend him, and may also fine the owner or trainer for whom he rode. *Engagements of Jockeys.*

(II) Employers retaining the same jockey have precedence according to the priority of their retainers.

(III.) Conflicting claims for the services of a jockey are to be decided by the Stewards.

83.   In the absence of a specified contract the fee for a winning mount shall be in all Steeplechases and Hurdle Races $50, and for a losing mount $25. For all races on the flat the fee for a winning mount shall be $25, and for a losing mount $10, unless specified by contract. *Jockeys winning and losing fees.*

STABLE EMPLOYERS.

84.   (I) In the absence of special agreement, engagements of riders, grooms or other attendants on horses in a racing stable terminates with the current year. *Engagements of Attendants on horses and effect of violating same.*

(II.) Any such person breaking his engagement shall not be allowed on the grounds of any association where these rules are in force.

(III.) No owner or trainer shall engage any such person who has not a written discharge from his last employer.

(IV.) Any person prevented by this rule from obtaining or retaining employment shall have the right of appeal to the Stewards of the National Steeplechase Association.

(V.) Any owner or trainer infringing this rule shall be fined not less than $100, and if he continue to employ or harbor such person after notice has been served on him by the late employer through the Clerk of the Course, either personally or by

letter addressed to his usual post office, he shall
be ruled off.

PART XXIII.

RACING COLORS.

85.   (I.) Racing colors shall be registered with the *Racing colors*
Jockey Club or with the National Steeplechase *shall be*
Association, either annually on payment of $1.00, *Registered.*
or for life of the person registering on payment of
$25.00. Colors so registered shall not be taken by
any other person. All disputes as to the right to
particular colors shall be settled by the Stewards
of the Jockey Club, or by the Stewards of the
National Steeplechase Association.

(II.) Any person running a horse in colors other *Running in*
than those registered in his own or assumed name *wrong colors.*
without a special declaration over night to the
Clerk of the Course (at a time prescribed) shall be
fined not less than $5.00 nor more than $10.00.

(III.) A special declaration is also required
where the owner is not the nominator.

(IV.) Jockeys must wear the colors of the owners *Number on arm*
of the horse, and a number on the arm or on the *or saddle cloth.*
saddle cloth (as may be prescribed by the
Stewards), corresponding to the number of the
horse as exhibited after weighing out.

(V.) Any deviation from the recorded colors of *Change of colors*
the owner that may be granted by the Stewards is *on Notice Board.*
to be immediately posted on the Notice Board.

(VI.) Under special circumstances a horse may *Under special*
be allowed to run in the name of the trainer, and *circumstances*
in colors not those of the owner. *changes may be allowed.*

PART XXIV.

DISQUALIFICATIONS OF PERSONS AND HORSES.

86.   (I.) If any person give or offer, or promise, *Bribes and bribe*
directly or indirectly, any bribe in any form to *taking.*
any person having official duties in relation to a
race or race horse, or to any trainer, jockey, or
agent. or to any other person having charge of, or
access to, any race horse ; or

(II.) If any person having official duties in relation to a race, or if any trainer, jockey, agent or other person having charge of, or access to, any race horse, accept or offer to accept any bribe in any form ; or

(III.) Wilfully enter, or cause to be entered, or to start for any race a horse which he knows or believes to be disqualified ; or *Knowingly entering a disqualified horse.*

(IV.) If any person be guilty of, or shall conspire with any other person for the commission of, or shall connive at any other person being guilty of any other corrupt or fraudulent practice in relation to racing in this or any other country. *Conspiracy to aid corrupt practices.*

Every person so offending shall be ruled off.

87.
(I.) Every person ruled off the Course of a recognized association is ruled off wherever these rules have force *Effect of being ruled off.*

(II.) When a person is ruled off, and so long as his exclusion continues, he shall not be qualified, whether acting as agent or otherwise, to subscribe for or to enter or to run any horse for any race. either in his own name or in that of any other person, and any horse of which he is the nominator, or is or was at the time of entry wholly or partly the owner, or which after one month from his exclusion shall be proved to the satisfaction of the Stewards to be, or to have been directly or indirectly, under his care, training, management or superintendence, shall be disqualified

(III.) If a horse run at any unrecognized meeting, he is disqualified for all races to which these rules apply. *Effect of running, training or riding at unrecognized meetings.*

(IV.) Any person acting in any official capacity and any owner or trainer running horses, and any jockey riding the same at any unrecognized meeting, shall be disqualified for all races to which these rules apply ; all other horses under the control of such owner or trainer shall also be disqualified.

PART XXV.

GENERAL POWERS OF STEWARDS.

88.   (I.) When there is no specified penalty for vio- *Stewards may*
lation of the rules or racing or of the regulations *disqualify, fine,*
of the course. the Stewards have power to disqual- *off.* *suspend or rule*
ify, fine, suspend, expell from or rule off.

(II) If any case occur which is not provided for
by these rules, it shall be decided by the rules of
The Jockey Club.   If no rule of The Jockey Club
is found applicable to the case, then it shall be
decided by the Stewards in such manner as they
may think just and comfortable to the usages
of the turf.

PART XXVI.

SPECIAL RULES FOR STEEPLECHASES AND HURDLE RACES.

89.   (I.) In Steeplechases and Hurdle Races, any *Horses getting*
horse getting away from his rider maybe remounted *away from riders*
in any part of the same field or enclosure in which *in Steeplechase or*
the occurrence took place, but should such horse *be remounted.* *Hurdle races may*
not be caught until he shall have entered another
field, then he shall be ridden or brought back to
the one in which he parted from his rider   Any
rider so losing his horse may be assisted in catching
him and remounting him without risk of disqualification; and in the event of a rider being disabled,
his horse may be ridden home by any person of
sufficient weight, provided he qualified according
to the conditions of the race.   No penalty shall be
exacted for carrying overweight in this instance.

Note.—In artificially constructed steeplechase
courses and in hurdle races the spaces between the
fences or hurdles are considered as fields or enclosures for the purpose of this rule.

II.   If any flag-post or boundary mark be placed *Riders must be*
in the course or altered after the riders have been *notified of*
shown over the ground, or had the course pointed *changes in any*
out to them, it shall not be considered binding or *course.*
of any effect unless such addition or alteration
shall have been particularly named, previous to
starting, to all the riders in the race, by one of the

Stewards, the Clerk of the Course, or by their
representatives.

III. If a horse refuse any fence or hurdle in a *Horses refusing.*
race, and it can be proved to the satisfaction of the
Stewards that he has been led over it by any of the
bystanders, or has been given a lead over by any
horseman not riding in the race, the horse shall be
disqualified.

PART XXVII.

HUNTERS' QUALIFICATIONS.

90. (I) No horse shall be qualified to start in races *Hunters must*
exclusively for hunters at meetings held under *have Certificate.*
these rules, unless with a certificate from the
National Hunt Association.

(II) Only persons holding licences from the *Gentlemen*
National Hunt Association as gentlemen riders, *riders.*
or qualified riders, will be allowed to ride as such
in races at meetings held under these rules.

PART XXVIII.

NEW RULES.

91.   No new rule of racing can be passed, nor can *Changes in rules*
any existing rule be rescinded or altered without *and proposed*
the proposed new rule, recission or alteration *new rules must*
being previously advertised three times in the *be advertised.*
Calendar, nor without notice being given in such
advertisement of the meeting of the Stewards
of the National Steeplechase Association at which
it is to be proposed, and no rule, recission or
alteration of a rule shall take effect until it has
been confirmed at the meeting ensuing that at
which it has been passed, nor until it has been
twice subsequently published in the Calendar.

PART XXIX.

FEES AND FINES.

92.   (I.) All fees and fines shall be paid to the *Fees and fines*
credit of the National Steeplechase Association, *must be paid to*
by the Association holding the meeting.   *National*
                                               Steeplechase
(II.) Fines must be paid within 48 hours ; *Association.*
delinquents may be ruled off the course.   *Fines in forty-*
93.   The following fees are also payable :   *eight hours.*

(I) The registration fee for horses shall be $2
for each horse. Such fee must be paid before
registration.

(II) For every registration of a foreign horse $5.

(III) For every registration of authority to act
generally on behalf of an owner, $1.00.

(IV) For every registration or change of an
assumed name, $15.00.

(V) For every registration of partnership. and
on every change thereof, $1 00 for each horse.

(VI) For every annual registration of colors
$1.00.

(VII) For every registration of colors for life,
$25.00.

(VIII) For registration of foreign and veterin-
ary certificates. $5.00.

(IX) For filing an agreement with a jockey,
$1.00.

(X) For collecting unpaid forfeits, five per
cent.

(XI) For change of name, $25.

(XII) For license to Jockey, $10 annually.

INDEX.

www.ingramcontent.com/pod-product-compliance
Lightning Source LLC
Chambersburg PA
CBHW021530270326
41930CB00008B/1184